Copyright © 2020 Tekkan
Artwork Copyright © 2020

All rights reserved.
First Printing, 2020
ISBN 978-1-7343510-8-8

To contact Tekkan please email:
buddhaboy1289@gmail.com

A poem by Cid Corman is on page 70.

for Darlene

How to Read My Poems

I have married the sonnet to the tanka. I tell a story in the sonnet — using three quatrains separated by line spaces, and a final couplet. The story builds to a conclusion in the couplet. The tanka is a commentary, or a counterpoint, to the sonnet — the combined poems have two endings.

I don't rhyme my sonnets, because I want freer expression. I want to be direct in my meaning — I want people to clearly understand my meaning. The metaphors are inspired by Shakespeare, and the (aimed-for) precision is in imitation of Japanese style. Using the sonnet with the tanka, I mix the sensibility of the Occident and the Orient — which I have done by living in England, Japan, and America.

I don't punctuate much in my poetry. I want the words themselves to do the work. There is logic between words, and the forms provide structure. By not using punctuation I hope to direct readers to carefully attend to each word — to appreciate the graininess of words.

Reading my poems silently, say, on a bus, a train, or an airplane, and reading them aloud, may be different experiences. The way I've written, there's not always a pause intended at the end of the line.

Hint: *My poems are to be recited not as lines but as phrases, and a phrase often overflows the break at the end of a line. I pause and take a breath where it seems natural for me to pause. Another person may pause differently than I do.*

Each single poem is a piece of a mosaic, and it is my hope that the collection of poems forms an accurate portrait of consciousness.

My daughter, Jocelyn MacDonald, is a wonderful artist. Her artwork graces this book.

I am Barry MacDonald. I received the *dharma* name *Tekkan*, which means "Iron Man," a settled practitioner of great determination.

— *Tekkan*

Everyday Mind XVII

The drizzle falling
slantwise in the wind
yesterday froze
onto my driveway
and sidewalk overnight.

We don't want to go inside because the
Virus is most contagious within rooms
And meeting online by video is
Not as good as person to person so

On Monday and Friday at about dawn
We ex-drinkers and addicts gather in
Pioneer Park on a limestone bluff with
A view of the wide and winding river

Southward and with downtown Stillwater
Beneath us and we can see the sun rise
The Crossing Bridge 3 miles in the distance
And the steel frame of the Lift Bridge below

As the few of us warm ourselves around
A fire in a portable container.

We each take a turn
we don't interrupt
we talk about being
free from addiction
and the joy of living.

Because yesterday was my 63rd
Birthday Darlene and I shared a cake and
She sang the birthday song and remarked how
Happy to be starting my 64th

Year which dampened my spirits because I
Was expecting that I would be having
Every month for 12 months the enjoyment
Of being 63 years old but no

Said Darlene who is better with numbers
As she patiently explained that at birth
We are 0 years old for 12 months and
Then we have our first birthday and begin

Living our second year which is very
Clarifying but also depressing.

I am older than
I thought I was
but not as smart.

What is the benefit of writing with
10-syllable lines making sure in the
Process that there aren't any extra words
Or phrases while being careful to be

Clear in meaning and to choose the exact
Word for a worthy idea because
I can't say that all of this falderol
Will produce better poetry or will

Elucidate the world more profoundly
Or poignantly than other poets do
But I excuse myself by saying that
I like playing the game that I'm playing

Am having a dump truck load of fun and
Poetry keeps me away from squabbles.

1 at a time
chickadees come
to the hedge outside
the window hopping
and darting away.

I have leveraged the uplifting joy
Of natural beauty to balance the
Dreary business of watching politics
Enclosing the squabbling human drama

Within the vibrations of the cosmos
But hatred and polarization are
Gaining momentum and the news is now
Political and it's increasingly

Difficult to trust the worthiness of
Media and I am frightened by the
Prospects of dictatorship confronting
Insurgency while I am determined

To find a sustaining poise transforming
Wrenching chaos into enlightenment.

A flock of birds
flew and settled into
high cottonwood branches —
a squirrel jumped
from the trunk to a branch.

Due to a spike in infection rates of
The pandemic virus and the sudden
Stress on hospitals doctors and nurses
The governor is closing restaurants

Schools and gyms again leaving me nowhere
To go for exercise in winter so
I bought a stationary bike in a
Box at Walmart and unpacked it in the

Living room and misassembled its parts
For several hours because instructions
Are usually boring and somehow
I managed to bolt everything backward

And upside-down making for myself a
Metal statuary of abstract art.

After exhausting
every mistaken
configuration
I persevered and
a bike has bloomed.

Before I bought the stationary bike
I thought economically and bought
A $3 jump rope and rolled up a
Portion of the rug in my living room

And learned that what was so easy 40
Years ago is not the same anymore
As my calf muscles and shins are not as
Springy with the 20 additional

Pounds to lift and even though in summer
I can race up the hill to Houlton on
My bicycle I realize today
That imitating the butterfly bounce

Of Muhammad Ali is a fancy
Better reserved for another lifetime.

The cycling motion
of the stationary bike
doesn't impact
my knees
and ankles.

The word from the governor is that gyms
Will be closed for a month but I believe
The closure will last much longer because
That is the pattern of pandemic and

Mandate so I went online to buy a
100-pound cast-iron dumbbell for
Use in my living room allowing me
To lift 100 times without stopping

With my back and left hand and then with
My right hand and I won't need the gym and
I'm saying goodbye to the gym where I've
Gone for 15 years and goodbye to my

Friends and I will miss our banter and
With whom will I complain about the news?

David owns the gym and
he's worked so hard and
renovated everything
and now maybe he'll
lose his business.

I don't believe anyone is to blame
As each of us brought opinions to the
Practice but I found myself leaving our
Saturday morning meetings upset and

Alienated and during the week
Before the next meeting I watched myself
Preparing verbal ammunition and
Arguing in my head and opposing

The most dominant figure in the group
And this pattern of agitation grew
Over years and is contrary to how
I want to practice meditation on

The way to waking up so I'm thinking
It's time to make a change of direction.

I am saying goodbye
to the group for now
surrendering arguments
seeking harmony
meditating.

I am aware that my profession of
Political commentary on 1
Level complicates my Buddhist practice
But on another I believe there is

A harmony to be discovered but
Recently I've watched as an entire
Network of national broadcast news has
Altered its ideology slowly

And now suddenly which is a scary
Consolidation of the replacement
Of balanced reporting with agenda
And propaganda news and I am sad

It's not possible for me to trust the
People I've listened to for many years.

How do I assimilate
watching shifting
balances of power
while pursuing
liberation?

I can see the many ways the world is
Evanescing into difference in
The ripping out of the road on the way
To the post office and in the paving

Of new asphalt and in the altercations
Of politics and the way those who I
Know talk about politics and in the
Way my friends and I aren't able to be

Friends in the nurturing way that once we
Were but it's more difficult to see the
Many ways that I am evanescing
Into difference as I am building

Defenses and seeking for other ways
In which nurturance is obtainable.

Anger is easy to see but
it's more difficult
to accept
grief and sadness.

In November the rain may plink and plunk
Upon the earth and then the air may freeze
And the rain becomes a dribble plunging
And spattering onto the windshields of

Cars and onto the streets and the walkways
And the drizzle stings the skin and sticks to
Concrete and asphalt making walking and
Driving slippery and dangerous and

Then the spittle may become the snow that
Doesn't have a predictable pattern
As it may blow sideways in a bitter
Wind or it may meander down gently

Circling in the tiniest of snowflakes
Caressing my face with teeny kisses.

If I didn't have to
move the snow from
driveways and
walkways maybe
I would like it.

In April Jason and I walked in a
State park and Jason bounds at a great pace
And we walked for a long distance over
Several days and on the morning after

The first day I discovered 3 of my
Toenails were black because my shoes were too
Tight and pinched which I ignored because I'm
Stubborn and they looked bad and I thought that

They would fall off but they didn't showing
Me that I don't know much about how the
Body operates as it decides
What to do without asking about my

Opinion so for 7 months I've been
Watching anticipating a result.

Funny ridges emerged
where the pristine growth
is pushing out and
I'm trimming off
the black nails.

There are many things to be heard in the
Hours before dawn when the distance is
Alive with vibrations and I did not
Notice it until suddenly I did

And could not determine from whence it came
As it emerged as a constant rumble
Weighty and throbbing in my ears and I
Realized that it was freight engine

Pulling quite a long train of cars in the
Country conforming to a schedule and
Proceeding to a destination and
Rolling deliberately over rails

Doing prosaic duty in the night
Mingling its rhythm with quiet darkness.

The quiet darkness
is pregnant with
life and
possibility.

I don't always feel at home in the world
And if I may make an analogy
I would compare myself to a fish who
Doesn't belong to any school of fish

Who indeed enjoys exploring the depths
Of the river and savors the deepest
And mysterious bottom wallowing
In the muck and then I do like slinking

Within and without of the warm rays of
The summer sun near the upper portion
Of the world but I am solitary
And I don't like being solitary

And once I feel winter enclosing me
With an icy grip I just yearn to leave.

I rouse myself
for a mighty effort
a leap of faith
and jump
out of my skin.

My going out of the house every day
And to the office is nothing new and
I wouldn't know how to live otherwise
But for Kitcat who spends every moment

In the house my leaving and shutting the
Door is the resumption of solitude
A solitude not of his choosing but
Imposed upon him for which I feel a

Little guilty and I wonder what he
Does when I'm not home but this morning he
Stared and pounced and swiped at the overlarge
Rabbit ears I was making while tying

Bootlaces and double knotting as if
To say go ahead and leave you big dope.

Returning home
driving onto my driveway
unlocking and opening
my door I see him
at the door.

The view outside of the window from the
Desk where I watch the sunrise and compose
Poetry and edit a journal of
Opinion is the background scenery

Of my consciousness so much better than
Looking at highways and strip malls as I
Can see bare branches in winter and
Foliage in summer backyards and middle

Class homes and through the bare trees the other
Side of the river valley during the
Winter and there comes a red juvenile
Squirrel who runs along the top of the

White wooden fence within easy sight and
He peppers my days with a dash of red.

Whatever opinions or
passions emerge into
my consciousness
arise from this
homely scenery.

Today is Thanksgiving Day which is a
Worthy tradition in America
But it can be tricky eliciting
An obligation to be grateful which

When one is burdened with a self-imposed
Sense of solitary weariness can
Instead summon a twinge of grievance but
I have only to flip a switch in my

Head to recognize my girlfriend and a
Stationary bike and a 100-
Pound dumbbell paid for with my property
Tax refund and morning clarity with

A view of the river valley and a
Little red squirrel to feel gratitude.

I am really grateful
that grumpy
obsession is only
temporary.

During this time of tribulation when
We are compelled to keep distance between
Each other because of the pandemic
Virus we meet online by using an

App called go-to-meeting which enables
Us with streaming video to appear
On screen from the comfort of our houses
And Glenn projects his image while sitting

In his garage with large sheets of plastic
Spread and looming about him that looks to
Me especially in the gloomy light
Like he is plopped in the middle of a

Huge net of cobwebs implying that in
The dark a giant spider is lurking.

I've warned Glenn
a bite from such a
garage spider
is worse than
the virus.

Even nightime dullness is pleasantly
Relaxing because I'm not expecting
Of myself that I have to accomplish
Anything so that I can lounge in bed

Reading about Tolkien's Middle-earth but
Morning is my favorite time of day
Because I can experience my mind
Waking up and extending probing thoughts

And it's not as if I need to lift a
Shield and grip a sword to make things happen
But when I feel my energy surging
With the sunrise then naturally there

Comes a purposeful enthusiasm
And everything I do becomes easy.

In the morning
I could mince a
garage spider
with a sword
without even sweating.

A kitchen knife is not a sword but it
Is handy for cutting celery and
Mushrooms and oranges and cashews to
Go with the turkey breast simmering in

The slow cooker as I was functioning
As the chopper and following Darlene's
Directions immersing myself in the
Simple task of slicing an onion with

A better method than I had known and
The delicacy of mincing garlic
Excludes extraneous thought reducing
The entire cosmos to what happens

Between my fingers the garlic and
The busy blade making such tiny bits.

On Thanksgiving day
Darlene and I had
a mushroom side dish —
breading — turkey — cranberries
pumpkin pie — whipped cream.

There is no snow on the ground now as we
Have had such a crazy season of snow
And thawing but the trees are bare and their
Branches and twigs look to be scratching a

Blue sky this morning and I'd have to be
Nuts to get on my bicycle when the
Air is cold and I do think about it
But I've got a stationary bike in

The living room separated from the
Buffeting wind and the challenging sight
Of the great distance ahead of me that
I have chosen in summer to traverse

Expending energy in becoming
A fleet pedaling racing animal.

I pinch my bicycle
tire on the way to the
living room where I
pedal while listening
to music.

A candle's flame is combusting in a
Gentle flickering fascinating to
Focus on as a metaphor for the
Daily expenditure of a lifetime's

Energy surrounded by the darkness
Of uncertainty and a purposeless
Striving so taxing and wearing down of
One's spirit over difficulty and

Time and what is a candle's flame besides
Oxygen molecules breaking down and
Moving quickly and appearing as a
Wavy glow on a wick supported by

A cylinder of wax filling a dark
Room with a weirdly cheerful tiny fire?

A lifetime's energy
is a miraculous
opportunity to
discover what
is joyful.

I do personalize uncertainty
Extending my probing thinking outward
Beyond my skin touching the 10 thousand
Things I can't control and beyond to the

10 million things my imagination
Cannot even conceive of yet and in
My yearning I address my questions to
A God of my understanding composed

Of molecules and sunlight and wind in
Winter trees and circumstances and the
Troubles I can't see around the corners
To timely solutions yet and so I

Pray for strength and optimism not in
Words so much but in gentle persistence.

Everything coming
to me and everything
proceeding from me
is a baffling and seamless
happening.

I am not going to say it's "nuts" to ride
My bicycle outside in the winter
Even upon November 28
Because it was warm enough and I saw

That the deer lying dead by the road in
Autumn has become a skeleton and
That the pebbles I avoided since the
Summer have been thrust aside by snowplows

And that the sun in late afternoon was
In a different place when I went west
Over the Crossing Bridge glaring at me
And obscuring my vision and I could

See that the vast river was becalmed and
Reflecting empty sky and wooded banks.

Again snow
melted and maybe
winter will not come.

How forgetful I am and grateful to
Be forgetful because if I were so
Burdened as to remember everything
That has happened I'd be comparing and

Second-guessing all of my behavior
And calculating and how difficult
It would be to be spontaneous and
Free from care but of all the events that

I could remember I have the habit
Of holding on to the painful and frightful
Memories creating an edited
Version of the past and playing the role

Of an unlucky victim steering me
Forward to repeat some of my mistakes.

Am I choosing
subconsciously
what to remember
what to forget?

The questions arise who is doing the
Remembering and the forgetting as
The pattern of life is going on and
Is there really a solid someone as

Stubborn as the Red Spot on Jupiter
Spinning like a perpetual whirlwind
Or is the collection of memories
And predispositions apparent now

Only a cherished illusion as a
Someone who is afraid of engulfment
Abandonment and nonbeing who clings
To life and clings with a terrified grip

Perpetuating needless suffering
And who is dissolving and emerging?

Maybe that's what
liberation means —
getting out from
under
me.

These pages are a fabrication of
Paper and ink and glue combined with the
Watercolor paintings and the pencil
Drawings of my daughter's artwork and the

Images and letters are presented
By computers and the books are formed by
A corporation relying on the
Internet for whatever profit may

Result and every book is assigned a
Number in a catalogue managed by
The Library of Congress recording
The efforts of millions of authors of

Billions of words each of whom propagates
A germ of the madness of a culture.

Our books are
like bubbles
compared with
Egyptian
hieroglyphics.

It is civilized to page through a book
To have the curiosity and peace
To absorb the harvest of a writer
And sit in a chair giving up the time

That could have been productive by doing
Something else so I am saying thank you
To anyone who happens on these words
And am disclosing that the methods I

Use were pioneered by Japanese and
British poets and today I'm making
A little joke as I am offering
You the everyday appeal of the hedge

Outside the window where chickadees are
Are stopping by hopping and saying hello.

I see the chickadee
the chickadee
sees me without
falderol.

The steel garage door was difficult to
Lift today and the wheels were in place and
The wire cables were OK but it took
Me a dozen heaves before I could make

It rise as if there were nothing wrong with
It and it wasn't jerky which to me means
That it doesn't need lubrication so
I'm at a loss to explain it other

Than to suppose that mechanical things
Behave strangely when suddenly the air
Plunges much colder than freezing as I
Can see steam rising from the chimneys of

Homes and a hoary frost is on the ground and
The folds of my jeans are cold and painful.

The sensations of
sudden bitter cold
are inevitable
in Minnesota.

The little squirrel runs along the top
Of the fence and the top of the fence curves
Up and down between the bigger posts that
Make the fence's framework so the little

Red squirrel runs up and down on the top
Of the fence and then it turns the corner
And it keeps running up and down and out
Of sight behind a shed and then a bird

Perhaps a sparrow flies to the topmost
Branches of a maple and perches for
A moment and then it flies away as
A time emerges when nothing happens

Until the squirrel is running up and
Down along the top of the fence again.

The white fence
outside my window
down a little hill
seems to be
important.

It is always the same sun exerting
A supremacy on the upward swing
Hypnotizing us with an illusion
Even though Copernicus revealed that

The earth is rotating on its axis at
1,000 miles an hour and the ground
Under our feet is moving and it takes
Me an effort to remember how much

Differently this same sun would appear
Rising over the Sahara blasting
The air burning the sand and compelling
Every living thing to adapt to its

Might as the sun smolders variously
Depending upon its proximity.

Trillions and trillions
of unseen suns
are swallowed
by vast
darkness.

The delivery on the sidewalk of
My 100-pound dumbbell presented
A chore as it was enclosed in cardboard
Without an easy grip so I lifted

It by prying my arms under and heaved
Up with my back and legs and plodded up
Onto the 2 concrete steps with a strain
And opened the doorknob with a twist of

A hand and a wrist swearing because of
The damn pandemic that made its online
Purchase necessary but I recalled
That the dumbbell is meant to uplift my

Spirit through exercise and that I should
Be ecstatic to get it off the ground.

The cast iron
instrument
sits on the
living room floor
with aplomb.

How much easier it is using a
Tough strip of cloth wrapping around a wrist
And the handle while bending at the hips
With a hand planted upon the coffee

Table to raise the dumbbell off the floor
And lift it rhythmically as often
As I can as the dumbbell and I are
Like a pair of synchronized swimmers with

Me pulling one direction my partner
Precisely the opposite without a
Smidgen of a gap coordinating
Without an instant's hesitation or

Perhaps we are performing a duet
Of muscular music and gravity.

Heaving a weight
isn't really a
form of art
it's an ordeal.

Driving on the way to the post office
I saw by the street in front of a house
Upon a tiny bit of grass between
The sidewalk and the house a flock of pink

Flamingos newly placed there on display
For the residents of Stillwater and
I marveled at the pluck of the owners
Who most certainly know that people think

The birds are crass and hideous and these
Are not the ordinary plastic things
But they are tastefully constructed in
Blocky fashion of either metal or

Wood a half-dozen of them perched within
A little spot looking quite exotic.

The flamingos constitute
the owner's personal
Declaration of
Independence.

I returned home for lunch and met Kitcat
At the door and I bustled about the
Rooms and didn't attend to Kitcat but
I saw him pawing insistently at

The closed curtains in my bedroom so I
Opened the curtains and the bright sunlight
Spilled into my bedroom and onto the
Comforter on my bed brightening and

Warming the room immediately and
Instantaneously Kitcat flopped on
The comforter with an attitude of
Supreme triumph stretching outward with his

Fore- and hindlegs extending his long spine
And then he relaxed in satisfaction.

With a brain the
size of a walnut
Kitcat is good at
manipulating me.

Kit and I communicate outside of
The bounds of organized language within
A range of emotive exclamations
Of grunts and woofs and I will employ a

Rising inflection for indicating
Questions and we have a working routine
Going in the morning after I rise
From bed when I will grab a metal-toothed

Brush and Kit will trot to the rug and flop
And I move him facing away from me
And brush vigorously and sometimes he
Will twist and seize the brush from me and

Manipulate the brush turning the brush
Upward on the rug and will comb his face.

Holding it with his paws
Kitcat moves his face
across the metal teeth
studiously.

I've been writing a lot of poetry
Lately because doing my business and
Attending to and commenting about
The news has been awful lately filling

Me with disappointment as the people
I used to trust are no longer worthy
Of trust as I am opposing what is
Happening in the world of people as

The narratives emanating from the
Studios and newsrooms are becoming
Increasingly intolerant of the
Opinions opposing their own as I

Believe the various media shills
Are establishing an Official View.

Writing about
a little red squirrel
a 100-pound dumbbell
and pink flamingos
is much easier.

We are sitting in lawn chairs circling the
Container of fire with only half of
The moon looming in the western sky and
With the sun clearing the horizon in

The east and I am attending to the
Conversation about living without
Alcohol but I'm also watching the
Ceaseless harmony of the orbs from the

Vantage of Pioneer Park seeing that
A half of the moon is invisible
Because the earth is blocking the sun from
Lighting it as daylight is brightening

All the unnumbered branches of the trees
And the bare branches are glowing orange.

Living without
alcohol helps me
get out from under
the stridency
of thinking.

There are newcomers to sobriety
Who are talking about relapse into
Alcoholism and the lying and
The desperation that go along with

A return to addicted drinking and
I am grateful to have them reminding
Me of the hangovers and the haze of
Mind that didn't lift till afternoon and

Each of us has the opportunity
Of becoming truly liberated
Bringing us together for more than the
Genuine comradery because

We want to practice principles and be
Honest and willing and open-minded.

I could be in bed
with a headache
instead of watching
the sun the moon
and bare branches.

I am wearing the same shirts over again
Washing them on occasion to remove
The coffee stains and to luxuriate
In the freshness of clean clothes and I am

Shaving because I do reveal my face
To people without a mask once in a
While in person and more often online
By video but the colder temps and

The separation of people due to
The ongoing pandemic is weighty
Pushing me to grumpy ruminations
While shut within my home putting me on

Guard against the emergence within me
Of a resurrected Neanderthal.

Isolation
encourages
uncivilized
masculine
tendencies.

I remember from the earliest years
Being allured and captivated by
The nurturing and the gentle grace of
The feminine other and there were dreams

Of surprising adolescent stiffness
And release under covers during the
Night but I learned not to talk about the
Imaginative attractions bursting

Upon me and I was hesitant and
Hindered by the low opinion that I
Already formed about myself serving
To magnify and exalt womanly

Beauty stimulating excitement and
Yearning but also filling me with doubt.

I was burdened
with secret lust
and obvious
awkwardness.

My adolescent inhibitions are
Mostly a thing of the past and I am
Much more comfortable and civilized in
Conversation with the opposite sex

In abiding by the societal
Boundaries in my observance of the
Courtesies of companionship and I
Am skillful in listening and happy

To learn from Darlene to chop onions to
Brown beef with a little coconut oil
And to make tacos but there is also a
Certain awareness that in relations

Between the genders at least in my case
Women will always have the upper hand.

I have about me
an irremediable
cloddishness and
a tinge of the
Neanderthal.

Besides playing with words I am also
Using a cryptic saying of Zen that
Is passed down through the centuries about
A question from a monk and an answer

By a master — what is the way of Zen? —
Your everyday mind is the way — which sounds
Quite simple but becomes tricky with the
Method being to study the self to

Forget the self and thusly to throw off
Body and mind and be enlightened by
The myriad things because I am moved
To have liberation from suffering

But the masters also say that force of
Will or cleverness cannot seize the goal.

I practice
intention
patience
awareness
daily.

Meditation helps to clear my mind and
Listening to recordings of Alan
Watts provides helpful signposts on the way
As I'm attending to the glimpses of

Insight contained within what the birds are
Doing and how the moon the sun and the
Earth are dancing together and how good
It feels to cut vegetables for a meal

With the intention of being clear in
My perceptions and accurate in my
Selection of words and nevertheless
Knowing that how I think the world works is

Quite different from how it does work and
The best that I can do is be playful.

The best I can do
is to skillfully
tame or leverage
agitation.

I just love listening to Alan Watts
Who calls himself a philosophical
Entertainer with the idea I
Suppose that one might as well have fun with

Ineffable conundrums as words
Are incapable of conveying the
Authentic insight — and the traditions
Of Zen are beside the point but the point

Is to be discovered either in 3
Seconds or in 30 years — and neither
In earnest effort nor in purposeful
Carelessness can the point be realized

But once a person is infected with
The germ of the *dharma* it's hard to quit.

How do you get
to where you
want to go when
you have already
arrived?

My 100-pound dumbbell squats on the
Floor in front of the couch and under the
Edge of the coffee table where it is
Out of the way and when I am watching

TV and wearing socks I like resting
A foot upon the gargantuan hunk
Of metal because it is a brutish
Thing over which I have total control

Within my sphere of domesticity
And I fancy myself a heroic
Big-game hunter lording over his prey
Except that the dumbbell is still alive

So twice a week I put on my wrist wraps
Hunker down and give the weight a trashing.

After we are done
taking only minutes
my body aches and
I put it on the floor
with satisfaction.

My sturdy metal stationary bike
Is also held within my living room
Positioned toward a window and just in
Front of the studio piano and

Waiting and appearing to me like a
Gazelle on the savanna and when I
Mount the beast for my daily indulgence
I picture myself a crouching lion

Pedaling at a precipitous pace
Listening to music on my headphones
Elevated 4 feet above the floor
At chest level and I'm regretting the

Scenery as I did like to watch the
Girls pass by my pedaling in the gym.

A joking engineer
manufactured
road reflectors
on the pedals of
a stationary bike.

I notice that when I am standing up
My eyes are always looking at the world
From exactly the same height no matter
Which direction I am looking though I

Do have boots with exceedingly high soles
And heels that transform my perspective and
When I am sitting or lying down the
World towers above me just so much as

The length of height that I've surrendered but
Most everyone is taller than me so
When I am squinting up at them they are
Gazing down upon me however if

We were standing together on the verge
Of the Grand Canyon it wouldn't matter.

It is about time
to return to the
optometrist
because I am not
seeing as I did.

Of all the perks of writing perhaps the
Most peculiar and addicting is the
Glimpse of insight that piques my interest and
Summons my curiosity which then

Compels a lust for articulation
Because the initial insight is a
Tasting of the original world that
Comes because I am poised to receive it

And because there are unnumbered angles
From which to approach any subject the
Playing with syllables and cadences
And ideas and words is a game without

End which is truly joyous even if the
The product amounts to total nonsense.

I have no
idea
today what
I will write
about
tomorrow.

It sometimes happens that a poem will
Have a tail that extends to another
Poem and I believe I've underplayed
The magic of the original world

Making it seem as though I myself were
The dynamo conjuring creation
Which isn't true and I more resemble
A sentient bubble on the way to

Bursting and the multidimensional
Vibrations carry on regardless of
My attitude as every second I
Question with sight and sound and taste and touch

And smell and the world answers precisely
With sight and sound and taste and touch and smell.

And persistent thought
meets its opposite
a pregnant
nothingness.

While walking on the Crossing Bridge across
The river valley in autumn I gave
Up believing that in this lifetime I
Would have the opportunity to meet

A partner to share my life with and I
Accepted a solitary future
Because there appeared to be too many
Complexities in the way of finding

Compatibility and on the next
Day Darlene sent me an email from a
A dating app that I forgot thinking
That no one would want to meet during the

Pandemic but I was mistaken and
Darlene and I are happy together.

Having an inside view
on another person's
life dissolves many
limiting
perspectives.

Sometimes waves of energetic thinking
Keep me simmering at 3 a.m. and
This morning I remembered the pivot
In my children's lives when they left our home

And began fending for themselves leaving
Me the duty of surrendering to
Them their birth certificates and Social
Security cards which I remembered

Obtaining for them at the consulate
In Osaka Japan where I arrived
By train and subway from Kyoto where
They were born and I ruminated at

Night would they be able to keep them safe
Because those documents can't be replaced?

Sometimes
the nagging
details of life
persist beyond
usefulness.

When nervous energy keeps me awake
At 3 a.m. I am not attending
To what is happening at the moment
But I am tangled in a net of thought

Either regretting the past or fearing
The future when I'd rather be sleeping
And I would be sleeping except that it's
Difficult sometimes to relax and let

Go of the urge to manhandle results
But eventually I do let go
Of trying to control everything as
It's a simple fact that I can't so the

Question arises how graceful can I
Be being patient with my impatience?

Letting go of thought
trusting beyond
appearances everything
is OK is a subtle
practice.

I'm looking at the back-cover photo
Of Cid Corman's thin book of poetry
AND THE WORD from which Cid is gazing at
Me looking to be in his 50s which

Is much younger than my memory of
Him from 30 years ago in Kyoto
With an elbow propped on a desk with a
Hand holding his bald head with sad humor

In his eyes and with a pensive smile and
Behind him are unorganized stacks of
Books reminding me of my own boxes
Of books and when perusing his sparsely

Worded poems again I recognize
His slowly articulated anguish.

Cid loved
words
seizing
whatever
meaning
he
could.

When they have something needing to be said
They use facial expressions opening
Their eyes wide or positioning their ears
And when their ears are flattened back it's clear

There is trouble about and then they may
Bark or bray or snort or huff or even
Bare teeth as they are social animals
Meandering in the treeless grasslands

Or the woodlands or southward upon the
Mountains moving in herds and keeping watch
For predators and when in danger they
May run in zigzag fashion or a male

May lower his head and outstretch his neck
Prepared to bite or turn around and kick.

Is the
zebra
white with
black stripes
or black
with white
stripes?

Their skin is grayish or muddy brown but
Underneath they are pink being rotund
And weighty with long barrel-shaped bodies
Culminating behind with a tufted

Little tail to go with tiny round ears
However their heads are gargantuan
And they are social animals living
Together in rivers and lakes and swamps

Able to hold their breath underwater
For 5 minutes wallowing in water
Most of the day communicating with
Wheezes and snorts and grumbles and booms and

Mostly they eat grass and fruit but they are
Extremely volatile and dangerous.

With little legs overland
a hippopotamus
can chase a human
as fast as 30
miles an hour.

They eat crustaceans and birds and frogs and
Fish and locusts not like anybody
Else because they can't chew or break apart
Smaller pieces of food so instead they

Swallow whole whatever they seize and they
Ingest small stones to help with grinding food
Within their stomachs and because of their
Slow metabolism they will live for

Months without eating a morsel which is
Comparable with what Hindu masters
Will do but unlike Hindus in colder
Months or during droughts they dig burrows in

The sides of riverbanks and clamber in
And hibernate or maybe meditate.

Crocodiles have
personalities like
agents of the
Internal Revenue
Service.

They have the largest eyes of any land
Animal and they each have 3 stomachs
And their legs are laughably skinny but
They sprint 43 miles an hour and

Run 31 miles an hour over
Distance while only having 2 toes on
Each of their 2 feet but running isn't
Their only defense as they can kill a

Lackadaisical lion with only
A single forward kick and their mating
Rituals are quite ritualized and
Synchronized with the male excitedly

Flapping alternative wings and with the
Female running circles around the male.

The flirty ostrich
reminds me of
John Travolta's
disco preening in
"Saturday Night Fever."

They spend most of their time underwater
Maneuvering for krill and squid and crab
Fleetly turning with stiff little flippers
And webbed feet having a thin layer of

Blubber and tightly packed oily feathers
For preserving warmth but upon the land
Their dignity is somewhat diminished
As they waddle and hop and run with their

Bodies bent forward and they toboggan
Sliding across the ice on their bellies
Pushing with their feet and for protection
And warmth they huddle into colonies

Of large and noisy anonymous mobs
As numerous as thousands or millions.

Penguins in mobs
remind me of reporters
at the annual
White House
Correspondents
Dinner.

These creatures possess the most sensitive
Organ of any mammal comprising
150,000 muscles and
Capable of picking up a peanut

And shelling it and blowing out the shell
And then maneuvering the nut to be
Eaten and the same organ can be used
As a straw or a snorkel and also these

Animals use the bottoms of their round
Flat feet to notice the low-frequency
Vibrations transmitted through the earth so
They can detect the slow rhythmic stomping

Of herds of fellow creatures 20 miles
Away and matriarchs govern the herds.

What a
marvel all
the abilities
of the elephant
are.

This animal is central to the health
Of the ecosystem as it keeps prey
From overconsuming vegetation
Thusly maintaining the balance of the

Streams and forests and even croplands and
Its tail is 3 feet long and provides poise
When making a sharp turn and this creature
Can swim long distances and its hind legs

Are longer than its front legs so it leaps
20 to 30 feet and it hunts deer
Wild boar buffalo antelope mostly
At night with vision 6 times better than

Human sight but it hunts successfully
Only once in 10 or 20 attempts.

The beneficent
tiger is best kept
at a respectful
distance.

Almost everyone thinks this animal
Is white but really its skin underneath
Is black and it is a marine mammal
Capable of swimming constantly for

Days paddling with large paws while holding
Its hind legs flat like a rudder and it
Has a prominent nose detecting prey
Over 3000 feet away and it

Spends half of its life hunting for bird's eggs
And seals and small mammals and even when
Possible vegetation but it is
Only successful in 2 percent of

Its efforts demonstrating it takes grit
To survive amidst the Arctic Ocean.

Polar bears
frolic in the
Arctic but not
in the Antarctic.

These birds have microscopic crystal-like
Formations in their feathers reflecting
Different wavelengths of light so that they
Shimmer like butterflies and hummingbirds

And when the male fans its tailfeathers they
Quiver emitting a low frequency
Vibration and depending on whether
The female is far or near the male may

Vary the sound by shaking different
Parts of the feathers and the female has
Sensors within her crest that are attuned
To receive the same frequency sent by

Humming male tailfeathers so that when he
Flickers his plumage he rattles her head.

The male is a peacock
the female a peahen
offspring peachicks
together they are
a bevy of peafowl.

It's a whimsical notion to propose
A network of consciousness within which
Every being sports a quality of
Awareness comporting with an array

Of abilities fitting hand in glove
With an environment and suppose that
We humans and each of us as nodes of
Consciousness have paid our dues by living

Multiple lifetimes as beings using
An eagle eye or a fish wiggle or
A butterfly flutter or a polar
Bear determination and suffering

Wolfish hunger monkey mind or bullish
Irascibility or a fly's death.

Have you never met
a predatory human
reminiscent of
a tick?

Humans make a pastime of stargazing
In the beginning watching stars without
Understanding the orbit of the earth
Around the sun and the rotation of

The earth on its axis but now we are
Sophisticated gauging the movements
Of planets within our solar system
Predicting that within days and upon

The longest night of the year the planets
Jupiter and Saturn even though they
Are hundreds of millions of miles apart
Will seem to converge in the south western

Sky near the horizon looking brilliant
And earning the name of the "Christmas Star."

It's been 800 years
from the Earth's view
since the conjunction
of Jupiter and Saturn
was so visible.

Sometimes I have wanted to be at an
Event that divergent circumstances
Prevented and then at other times I've
Been to meetings where I wished afterward

That I did not attend for example
There were years of writing groups taking place
With Cid Corman after I left Kyoto
Japan and came to America that

I missed and on the other hand I would
Rather not have met the BMW with
My Corolla in the smash accident
On a side street in Minneapolis

As so often it seems that I was where
I was but wasn't happy to be there.

While planets keep
appointed places
my movements
are unpredictable.

Cid would read poems from ancient China
From America from correspondence
Would talk about when a crippled poet
Embarrassed and brought to earth a prig of

A poet and would dwell on the hardships
Of people he knew of turnings and dead
Ends demonstrating that writing only
Works when it tells the truth and it has an

Impact as about his enuresis
The unconcealable smell of sleeping
Sitting in his own piss which wasn't the
Terror but was in fact comfort and warmth

But always he heard Mother cursing Dad
Alone in the night hearing that door slam.

Lying in bed
thinking about
Cid I also hear
that door slam.

Every other Sunday for several
Years Cid led a poetry workshop in
My living room 30 years ago and
I considered how dissimilar we

Appeared and I reacted against his
Unwarranted pessimism as I
Believed with a doubtful optimism
But I looked forward to his baritone

Rambling even his tough assessment of
My writing because he had a hungry
Sincerity and intimate knowledge
Of the centuries of poetry and

He turned his egoism into a
Unappeasable thirsting for meaning.

Today
Cid Corman
influences
the leverage
of my words.

This poem was found
on a folded piece of paper
with Cid's looping signature
inside a book of Cid's poetry:

**WORK
SHOP
TALK**

There is of course a
word — <u>the</u> word. Think — feel —
become exact — be

at the point of it
point — going in the
direction you go.

—*Cid Corman*

I've been playing with dreams lately trying
To summon the will at poignant moments
To rise from bed and turn on the lights to
Scrawl words upon paper as a record

To ponder later and during daylight
I've been musing whether my visions at
Night are the spark of my unconsciousness
Inflaming my subconsciousness in turn

Subliminally cooking my walking-
Around mentality or whether these
Terms of psychology are really just
The idle mumbo jumbo of a few

Creative cranks and that dreams are only
Vibrations on another frequency.

Even in my dreams
I discover myself
striving
dubiously.

I don't remember being nobody
And the word "nobody" is a trick
When used in deprecation of someone
Who is contriving to be somebody

And it's difficult to be accurate
When saying "nowhere" because everything
Is residing in a place relative
To somewhere else and even beyond the

Sky the galaxies have their neighborhoods
And perhaps the most paradoxical
Label of all is "nothing" because it
Negates everything that so clearly is

And there isn't anything that isn't
Busy doing something going somewhere.

But once I was
nobody
nowhere
in the middle of
nothing.

What a burden in adolescence to
Be inflicted with acne dreading to
Look in the mirror and spot a fresh bloom of
Pustules boils or blackheads overnight when

Blossoming into self-consciousness is
A gauntlet of self-criticism and
Doubt generating a compulsion of
Comparison with the fortunate youth

Who have confidence and enchanting skin
During the critical seasons when the
Opposite sex is so mysterious
And comely when looking attractive is

Paramount then to be mortified and
Exposed to gossiping competitors.

I sometimes
envied dogs
with
furry faces.

Among the first words a child learns is "no"
Which is an omnipotent word but when
Coming from a mother its meaning is
Leavened with love intending only the

Safekeeping of the child but as life was
Happening into adolescence and
Adulthood the inconvenient hardship
Of having to hear the word repeated

And of having to endure rejection
In all the ways that "no" is not spoken
But apparent how agonizing it
Was for me — for myself — to find my

Balance to accept denial as a
Direction and not as a negation.

Learning how
to relax and not
care too much
is tricky.

A few of us are continuing to
Meet even as the temperature is
Getting colder and the darkness of night
Is lengthening as the winter solstice

Is approaching and we are stubbornly
Gathering in Pioneer Park huddled
Around a fire in a portable
Container and we are not wearing the

Prescribed masks during this vile pandemic
Season trusting to luck to a prudent
Distance we are keeping from each other
Dedicated as we are watching the

Sunrise savoring our happy talk and
Braving the happenstance of a rogue sneeze.

We are rebellious
primitives who didn't
bother building
Stonehenge.

There are those few occasions when after
Meditating I discover that I'd
Forgotten to push the button on the
Coffeemaker and that somehow I had

Sat for 40 minutes oblivious
To the absence of the bubbling brew and
The delicious aroma coming from
The kitchen next to the living room that

I love so much that somehow after years
Of practicing mindful awareness that I
Didn't manage what was most important
And that then belatedly I have to

Push the button afterwards and dawdle
Because I can't leave home without coffee.

I wonder whether
the Buddha was
ever impatiently
forgetful or if it's
just me.

I wonder what wry attitude someone
Would adopt looking at the life I am
Living which I myself believe is 1
Of burdensome complexity when what

They would observe is my useless sitting
On a cushion every morning followed
By my dawdling over poetry for
The most creative hour of the day

After which I deign to squeeze in a bit
Of work which is the only thing I'm paid
For — commenting on the news — and then there's
Lunch with "talk radio" and then a bit

More work in the afternoon leading up
To a lusty session of exercise.

It is an
impractical
solid-as-a-bubble
odd assortment
of doings.

It's a weighty question whether to put
Faith in linear time with a defined
Beginning and an uncompromising
Ending followed by an eternity

Of an uncertain locality or
Whether to allow oneself to be caught
Up in the swirl of cyclical timing
Comporting with the orbits of planets

The seasons of the year and the circles
Of the galaxies and the questions may
Be asked are the galaxies quickening
In a straight line away from the Big Bang

To lose energy and to dissipate
And then may the Big Bang happen again?

Is the questioning
remembering
forgetting person
a bubble that keeps
popping and bubbling?

Since I have made such a big deal about
Saying everything is busy doing
Something and going somewhere a person
May ask — what does a rock do? — and I say

A rock is lying on the ground or in
The ground and it is also moving in
4 directions at the same time with the
Earth rotating on its axis and with

The earth orbiting the sun and with the
Solar system orbiting the Milky
Way and even the Milky Way as a
Spiraling assemblage of a mob of

100 thousand million stars is in
A stupendous hurry going somewhere.

The Milky Way is
zipping 1.3 million
miles an hour to
who knows where?

On behalf of the livelier beings
Of the earth I would like to express my
Gratitude for rocks for the quiet and
The underlying and unacknowledged

Support that the rocks are providing us
Everyday in their variety as
Granite gabbro basalt limestone marble
Slate and shale in their evolution as

Igneous rocks that are molten and then
Cool as metamorphic rocks that are formed
By persisting heat and pressure and as
Sedimentary rocks that are scattered

Pieces of other rocks that are moved by
The wind water ice and biology.

Every pebble and
grain of sand has a
pedigree
originating
in mystery.

It wasn't immediately clear to
Me that 1 day I would appreciate
The taste of a dill pickle because in
My initial experience I do

Remember only its astringency
Compelling me to stretch my face in a
Kind of grimace and shut my eyes as an
Involuntary act of a futile

Avoidance so opposite was its tang
From say vanilla ice cream but don't ask
How my attitude changed or even why
I ventured another bite but doing

So brought me to an eventual point
Of admiration for its sharp appeal.

Maybe a clever
inventor is working
on a salmon
or a trout
ice cream?

I put it inside my mouth
and tasted it with my tongue
I contorted my face
And wrinkled my nose
The damage already done.

It is the Christmas season for giving
Gifts and for imagining what those who
Are on my list would find joy in maybe
A Star Wars or a Lord of the Rings thing

Comporting with particular passions
Or perhaps it's better to give useful
Gifts like kitchen knives or French berets for
Minnesota blizzards but this year I

Have propelled through the post office missiles
Of a strange and dubious quality
Inside of envelopes comprising a
Book of poetry written by me that

May be incomprehensibly dull to
Those who don't covet my odd obsessions.

Sometimes books
only serve to hold
other books upright
on shelves gathering
dust.

Jason told me the winter solstice passed
This morning at 4 a.m. which was a
Surprise as I had thought it would happen
Tomorrow and this morning the sky is

A gloomy gray and the landscape is a
Drab mixture of bare branches and lifeless
Grass without a covering of snow which
Is not typical and less cheery for

The season but I'm happy because there
Will be more daylight and less darkness from
Today and I am jaunty because I'm
Part of the vast cycle of the seasons

Accepting a gloriously gloomy
Day with the sun resplendent behind clouds.

The convergence of
Jupiter and Saturn
in the south western sky
may pass unseen tonight
by Minnesotans.

On the evening of The Great Conjunction
When Jupiter and Saturn converge in
The south western sky that also happens
To coincide with the morning of the

Winter Solstice the frictionless motion
Of the planets of our solar system
May be aligning and diverging in
Ceaseless dances about the sun but in

Minnesota we stargazers are stuck
Waiting for the forecasted clearing of
The clouds which given the iffy nature
Of day-to-day meteorology may

Or may not occur any minute now
As I am waiting with my fingers crossed.

Apparently the
daily weather
is harder to gauge
than planetary
orbits.

I'm able to see electric Christmas
Lights outside of the window now but not
The south western sky where I may or may
Not see The Great Conjunction which hasn't

Happened so uniquely in 800
Years so I'll take the occasion now to
Tear myself away from writing about
Wonderment when I could instead be a

Witness to the event so I will drive
To Hardee's family restaurant to
Order some takeout sandwiches to tide
Me over for the week and determine

Whether the Great Event is visible
And to escape the bother of cooking.

If we were Martians
living on the arid plains
of Mars the evening
would be a
nonevent.

I got the sandwiches but the planets
Converged out of sight beyond a layer
Of clouds and while driving I noticed a
Tinge of congestion and then a touch of

The sniffles prompting a remembrance
Of the occasional cough this morning
In Pioneer Park precipitating
A twinge of apprehensive questioning

About whether I was facing a cold
Or COVID-19 but such tweaking of
Doom didn't keep me from the satisfied
Consumption of 2 sandwiches nor did

It hinder my phone conversation with
Darlene while I was lying on the couch.

But on rising from
the couch I went on a
tear of vertigo that
caused me to
trip about.

My situation last night was not a
Comedy of a tinge of vertigo
But a whack of wooziness which left me
Wondering what to do beyond sleeping

Anticipating accelerating
Deterioration of my condition
Including a fever and nausea
And disorientation and fatigue

And chills compelling a separation
From people and a cessation of work
Which are what so many people about
The globe are experiencing but I

Mostly feared a constriction of my breath
A not-funny-at-all suffocation.

But beyond
a tinkle of
lightheadedness
this morning
I'm OK.

It's an ongoing tradition in May
In Japan to write poetry about
Cherry blossoms as they are fetching and
Delicate blooms brightening all the parks

After a season of barrenness but
It's tricky after so many years of
Creativity to find something new
To say so in Minnesota and in

December I will celebrate with a
1-of-a-kind tree in Pioneer Park
Diminutive and humble compared with
The surrounding trees but as closely as

I look there's no indication of a
Hint of the coming of cherry blossoms.

Absent cherry blooms
are a hint of the
emptiness
producing
everything.

Cherry blooms after winter year after
Year remind me of the resurrection
Of loveliness and winter solstice pricks
My consciousness of brighter days coming

Though January and February
Are months of bitter cold and piercing wind
As blizzards blow across Minnesota
As icy roadways become dangerous

And once Christmas and New Year's Day are done
Winter resembles a weary trudge through
The tundra where the city snowplows and
A homeowner's snow blower are symbols

Of determined resistance and mittens
Knitted hats and boots are magnificent.

The corners at the
end of my driveway
will become heaped
with piles of snow
higher than me.

Yesterday evening the clouds disappeared
And Jason sent me a photo by way of
The Internet taken I suppose by
His smartphone of the unconverging of

Saturn and Jupiter which will happen
Gradually day by day and I saw
A speck of light which isn't the light of
The planets themselves but is a fleck of

Sunlight ricocheting off the planets
And back to earth captured by a smartphone
And transmitted by email and into
The jewels of my eyes and now I feel

A little guilty I didn't have the
Gumption to see the sight honestly.

What impresses
is the vast
enveloping
darkness
unveiled
every night.

I am listening to the vibrations
Inside of the ear canals while I am
Sitting in a chair hearing the pumping
Of the heart as a rhymical thumping

And feel blood throbbing in the veins of the
Arms and legs and I am taking part in
The inflow of air in the nostrils and
Swelling the lungs with oxygen holding

For a moment and then releasing and
Can focus an awareness inside of
Each of the pinkie toes and fingers to
Sense pulsation and can extrapolate

While typing that the nails of the fingers
Need trimming but maybe not the toenails.

The pulsation of sunlight
even on a cloudy day
merges with the
throbbing of the
heart.

At 11 a.m. I listen to
Talk radio tuning in with the news
And the personality I like is
Expert at political scheming and

At characterizing politicos
And like everyone else commenting on
Politics there's a wallop of disgust
And ridicule and the listeners and

The host are equally caught up in the
Mission of defeating the other side
And the hangover from the election
Makes us feel defeated and desperate

With an unhealthy dose of betrayal
That is hard to hear and hard to turn off.

Listening to
or reading the
news is an out-
of-the-body
experience.

I gave my 100-pound dumbbell a
Kick but it proved to be unmovable
Upon the floor and I'm not intending
To engage with it until tomorrow

As it becomes a weight in the back of
My mind a day before our mutual
Involvement and in between our sessions
Of exercise I do admire its

Simplicity and brutal symmetry
Resting on the floor of my living room
Looking like a dwarvish piece of modern
Art complementing the stationary

Bike giving the chamber of my man cave
An ambience of steel barbarity.

I keep it under the edge
of the coffee table
enough out of the way
so as not to stub a
toe in the dark.

The ground a couple days before Christmas
Is without snow but it is raining now
And soon this afternoon it will drizzle
And then begin to snow and as it descends

The temperature will plunge to bitter
Cold forcing me onto my toes waiting
To make a calculation whether I
Can move the heavy wet most difficult

Type of snow off of 2 driveways before
The wind turns icy and the cold becomes
Unbearable as we have been lucky
Up to now but there's no escaping the

Eventuality of confounding
Recurring enveloping Arctic slop.

Where do the
crows and the
chickadees
shelter?

Winter lies dormant for half of the year
In Minnesota and for much of this
Winter we've been blessed with little snow and
Mild temperatures but over many

Seasons of blizzards I've developed a
Yet unrecognized malady of Post-
Traumatic February Disorder
In which the snowfalls from November through

April merge in the mind of a person
Into 1 weary phenomenon of
Shovel snow blower and city snowplow
Repeatedly playing over again

Disturbing even nighttime repose with
Dreams of shovel snow blower and snowplow.

From November through April
the threat of February
is just below the surface
poised
to emerge.

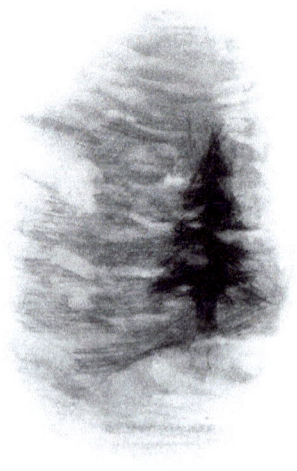

There are stages in the passage of a
Blizzard that are not at all unpleasant
Like when the wind is howling and icy
And the snow is zipping sideways in the

Wind and nothing is visible outside
Of the window except the blowing snow
And the temperature has plunged below
0 when I have warm exuberant

Gratitude for owning a furnace in
The basement and for using the curtains
Of my windows and for my electric
Light bulbs enabling me to don a

Bathrobe to close the curtains to savor
The heat and to watch a nonsense movie.

Then the world outside
the window does not
exist and there is no
February.

A reckoning comes the morning after
When I step outside the door into the
Snow and gauge the depth of the ordeal
And yes the cold was bitter today so

I donned 2 knitted hats the moon boots the
Elephantine mittens and the quilted
Long underwear girding my body for
Battle but firstly I noticed the wind

Had blown the snow off of the roof so the
Snow rake wasn't necessary and
The drifting snow wasn't deep and because
The cold came suddenly the snow wasn't

Wet and heavy but was fluffy and my
Snow blower works at its best in the cold.

My driveway
wasn't difficult but
an obstacle loomed —
my mom's
snow blower.

I yanked on the cord to start the other
Snow blower for my Mom's driveway over
30 times on 4 separate tries with
No success and before it has helped to

Be patient and to try again later
But this time I gave up while thinking of
My brother-in-law because he is a
Magician with machines and maybe he

Can fix it even though this blower is
Cantankerous and is more than 20
Years old and works well after it starts but
Getting it started is much more than a

Secondary detail because nothing
Happens without a propitious yank.

I'm a wordy guy
who has gotten through
many winters by
merely yanking
on cords.

Fresh fallen snow
on the day of
Christmas Eve
does look
magnificent.

—*Tekkan*

www.ingramcontent.com/pod-product-compliance
Lightning Source LLC
Chambersburg PA
CBHW042118100526
44587CB00025B/4101